Nanette Newman's
NEW
FUN FOOD FACTORY

If you think you'd like to learn a bit more about cooking — and make things that will surprise everyone — then this is the book for you.

Sign on for this special cookery course just for you.

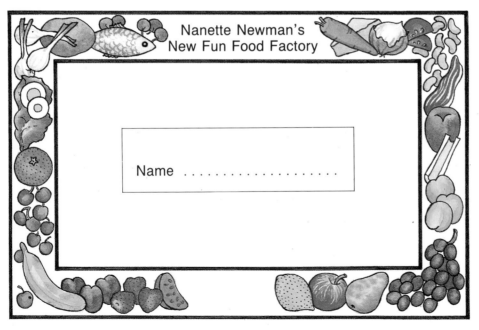

Nanette Newman's
New Fun Food Factory

Name . . . .

Nanette Newman's
NEW
FUN FOOD FACTORY

Written and compiled by Nanette Newman
Illustrated by Mary Cooper

Studio Publications
Ipswich, England

CONTENTS

© 1987 Studio Publications (Ipswich) Limited

Printed and bound in Great Britain

The recipes in this book have been tested and approved by qualified Home Economists, under the supervision of The Department of Catering and Fashion, at the Suffolk College of Higher and Further Education, Ipswich, Suffolk.

Notes to Factory Members

Exciting Bits
Apart from the fun of cooking, you will be making something that your friends and family will enjoy. You could give a party and do all the cooking yourself or cook dinner for your mother or father as a special treat or bake a cake as a present for someone special.

Important Bits
Never let younger children help you cut up things or take hot things off the stove or out of the oven.
Be careful when using kitchen gadgets — they can be dangerous. Only use a machine if you've got permission.

Fun Bits
Use the plastic shaped liners from chocolate boxes as moulds to make fancy ice lumps. Do use a tray to carry them! Don't throw away empty yoghurt or egg cartons. Use them for growing herb seeds in.

Sensible Bits
If you want to slice an onion without crying, peel it and put it in to the freezer compartment of the fridge for ten minutes, before cutting it up.
If you lie a cream cracker on a slice of bread while buttering it, it won't break.

Boring Bits
Try not to be too messy. A clean kitchen means they'll let you cook again.

Remember — Only use ingredients that are fresh and natural. Nothing artificial — no preservatives, colourings or flavourings, nothing out of a tin. Use wholemeal flour, brown sugar, sunflower oil and brown rice whenever possible.

Factory Rules

- Make sure you have permission to cook from the factory manager (usually called a mother), or whoever owns the kitchen.

- Always wash your hands first.
Remember that hot things can burn you, fat can spit at you, knives can cut you, and boiling water can scald you — look out for this sign

- Be careful when using kitchen gadgets — they can be dangerous — and never touch an electric plug with wet hands.

- Get all the right ingredients together before you start.

- Never waste food. It is expensive.

- Wear an apron or overall to protect your clothes.

- Clear up after you.

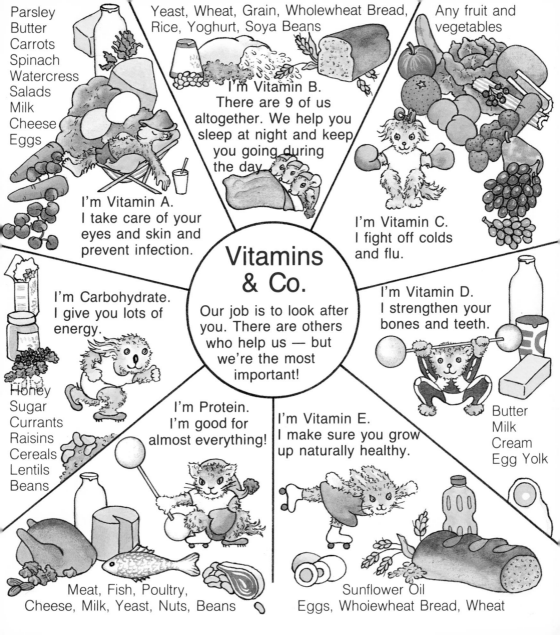

Parsley
Butter
Carrots
Spinach
Watercress
Salads
Milk
Cheese
Eggs

I'm Vitamin A.
I take care of your
eyes and skin and
prevent infection.

Yeast, Wheat, Grain, Wholewheat Bread,
Rice, Yoghurt, Soya Beans

I'm Vitamin B.
There are 9 of us
altogether. We help you
sleep at night and keep
you going during
the day

Any fruit and
vegetables

I'm Vitamin C.
I fight off colds
and flu.

Vitamins
& Co.

Our job is to look after
you. There are others
who help us — but
we're the most
important!

I'm Carbohydrate.
I give you lots of
energy.

Honey
Sugar
Currants
Raisins
Cereals
Lentils
Beans

I'm Vitamin D.
I strengthen your
bones and teeth.

Butter
Milk
Cream
Egg Yolk

I'm Protein.
I'm good for
almost everything!

I'm Vitamin E.
I make sure you grow
up naturally healthy.

Meat, Fish, Poultry,
Cheese, Milk, Yeast, Nuts, Beans

Sunflower Oil
Eggs, Whoiewheat Bread, Wheat

Your Own Breakfast Recipe

You will need........

4 handfuls Oatmeal
1 large handful Dessicated
Coconut
1 very small handful Mixed Nuts
1 handful Wheatgerm
1 dessertspoon Sunflower Oil
3 dessertspoons Honey
1 dessertspoon Brown Sugar

How to........

1. Mix everything together in a bowl.

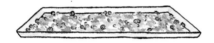

2. Then spread on a lightly oiled baking tin.

3. Bake at 350°F/180°C, Gas 4. Every 5 minutes move it around with a fork until it gets brown and crunchy.

You can store it in a jar and you can add chopped dates, dried apricots or raisins.
Then eat it with yoghurt for your breakfast.
(When making the muffin recipe, use your own breakfast cereal instead of a bought one in the recipe.)

8

Anytime Muffins

You will need........

9 oz (252 g) Wholewheat Flour
4 oz (112 g) Brown Sugar
4 oz (112 g) crunchy Breakfast Cereal
3 level teaspoons Baking Powder
¼ teaspoon Salt
1 Egg
½ pint (300 ml) Milk
⅛ pint (75 ml) Oil
2 tablespoons of any of the following — chopped apple or chopped banana or chopped nuts or sultanas

(Eat them as they are, or with butter and honey.)

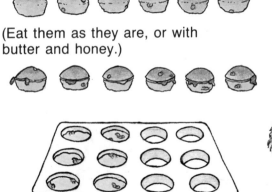

How to........

1. Put flour, cereal, sugar, baking powder and salt in one bowl.
In another bowl beat egg, add milk and oil. Add dry ingredients.
Mix and add your fruit or nuts.

2. Grease 12 muffin or patty tins. Spoon some of the mixture into each one (not quite to the top).

3. Bake at 400°F/200°C, Gas 6 for 20 to 25 minutes.

9

Instant Lunch or Snack Ideas

Strawberry Crunch

How to........

1. Mash up 6 large strawberries (or other fruit). Stir into a strawberry yoghurt.

2. Add 2 tablespoons of your favourite crunchy cereal.

Cheesy Pear

How to........

Cut a large pear in half. Scoop out the core gently and fill with cottage cheese sprinkled with chopped nuts.

Wholesome Slice

How to . . . .

On top of a thick slice of wholemeal bread, spread some mayonnaise, top with grated carrot, a peeled orange cut in chunks, a few sultanas and sprinkle with salted peanuts.

I-Spy Fry

How to . . . .

1. Cut a hole in a large slice of bread with a pastry cutter.
Gently melt 1 tablespoon of butter in a saucepan.
Fry bread on one side, turn over.

2. Break an egg into a cup, then gently slide the egg into the hole in the bread. Cook over low heat till the egg is done to your liking. Remove with a fish slice (a bit tricky) on to a plate.

11

Vegetable Soup for Two

You will need........

2 Carrots, peeled and chopped
1 medium Onion, peeled and chopped
1 medium Potato, peeled and chopped
2 tablespoons Frozen Peas
½ oz (14 g) Butter
¾ pint (450 ml) Chicken Stock
(crumble a chicken stock cube into ¾ pint (450 ml) boiling water)
1 dessertspoon Rice
1 teaspoon Parsley, chopped
2 sticks of Celery, chopped

How to........

1. Melt butter in a large pan.
Add onion and stir around for a minute.
Add carrot and celery and stir around for another minute.
Remove from heat.

2. Carefully, add the stock and return to heat.
Add potato and rice.
Simmer over a low heat for about 30 minutes or until all the vegetables feel soft when prodded with a fork. Add a little water to thin, if necessary. Add peas and cook for 3 minutes more.

To serve, ladle into bowls, sprinkle with parsley and eat with a big slice of bread.

(Experiment with other vegetable combinations. Try cauliflower, courgette or parsnip, or use tiny pasta shells instead of rice.)

12

Great Gazpacho

You will need........

4 oz (112 g) finely chopped Tomato
2 oz (56 g) finely chopped Celery
2 oz (56 g) finely chopped Spring Onion
2 oz (56 g) finely chopped Cucumber
2 oz (56 g) finely chopped Red,
Green or Yellow Pepper
2 teaspoons chopped Chives or
Parsley
Put in large bowl and stir.

3 tablespoons Wine Vinegar
2 tablespoons Oil
1¼ pints (750 ml) Tomato Juice
½ teaspoon Salt
½ teaspoon Worcestershire Sauce
¼ teaspoon Pepper
Put in bowl and stir really well.

How to........

1. Pour tomato juice mixture into the bowl with the vegetables. Stir well. Add two teaspoons of chopped chives or parsley.

2. Cover and leave in fridge to chill (you can leave it overnight).
Serve very cold with chunks of crusty bread.

(You can try adding some fresh herbs too.)

13

No-Cook Tomato Soup

You will need........

2 lb (896 g) Tomatoes
1 level teaspoon Salt
Juice of 1 Lemon
1 oz (28 g) Sugar
1 teaspoon Worcestershire Sauce
Small tub of Single Cream

How to........

1. Chop tomatoes and whirl in a blender.

3. Add everything else and whisk until well blended. Chill well in refrigerator before serving.
(If you don't like cold soup, heat very gently over a low heat, but make sure it doesn't boil.)

2. Then press through a sieve (this will make sure you have all the pulp and juice with no pips).

Special Vegetables

You will need.......

1 cup grated Carrot
1 cup shredded White Cabbage
1 cup shredded Red Cabbage
½ cup Celery, cut in thin strips
2 tablespoons Oil
1 dessertspoon Vinegar
½ teaspoon Salt
¼ teaspoon Pepper

How to.......

1. Heat oil in a large, wide pan. When hot, add carrot, cabbage and celery. Turn up heat a little and stir, adding salt and pepper.

2. Add vinegar and cook for about 2 minutes whilst stirring.

Serve immediately.

15

Home-Made Bread

You will need........

3 lb (1½ kg) Wholewheat Flour
2 oz (56 g) Butter
½ oz (14 g) Dried Yeast
+ 1 heaped teaspoon Brown Sugar
1½ (900 ml) pints Tepid Water
1 tablespoon Salt
2 level tablespoons Brown Sugar

How to........

1. Mix ½ pint tepid water with 1 teaspoonful of sugar. Stir in yeast. Leave in a warm place for about 10 to 15 minutes (it will start to bubble).

2. In another bowl, rub flour and butter together with your fingers.

3. Put 2 tablespoons of sugar into 1 pint of tepid water in a jug, stir till sugar is melted and add this to the flour. Add yeast mixture and salt. Mix with your hands and keep on doing this for about 5 minutes.

4. Keep on pushing, pounding, turning, hitting until it feels quite smooth (this is called kneading).

16

5. Put dough in a bowl, cover with a tea-cloth and put somewhere warm for 40 minutes.

6. Then remove dough and push and pummel again.

7. Divide the mixture into two pieces. Put it on to two greased baking tins. Leave dough to rise again for 20 minutes.

8. Bake at 400°F/200°C, Gas 6 for 45 – 50 minutes. Bread is cooked if it sounds hollow when tapped on the bottom.

(Make your bread into any shape that you like.)

17

Birds' Nests

You will need........

1 large Potato (half per person)
1 Egg per person
Salt
Pepper
¼ pint (150 ml) Milk
1 dessertspoon grated Cheese
1 dessertspoon Chives or Parsley
1 dessertspoon Butter

How to........

1. Scrub potato clean, dry and rub a little oil into skin. Prick skin with fork.

2. Bake at 375°F/190°C, Gas 5 for about 1 hour. Potato should feel soft when pressed.

3. Cut in half carefully.

4. Scoop out potato with spoon and put in bowl.

5. Add milk, salt, pepper and butter. Mash well.

18

6. Divide mixture into each potato shell and make a hole in centre of each mound of potato.

7. Then mark with fork to look like a nest. Carefully break an egg into each hole.

8. Sprinkle with cheese or herbs and place on baking tin.

9. Cook under grill or bake in oven at 350°F/180°C, Gas 4 until eggs are set the way you like them.

(Serves 2)

19

Crazy Cabbage

You will need. . . . . . .

12 Large Cabbage Leaves
Mixture of any of the following,
adding up to four large cupfuls:
Carrots
Peas
Parsnips
Spinach
Leeks
Onions
Cabbage
Beans
Brussel Sprouts
Potatoes
(All cooked and chopped up)

3 Eggs
4 oz (112 g) grated Cheddar
Cheese
⅓ pint (200 ml) Milk
½ teaspoon Salt
¼ teaspoon Pepper
1 dessertspoon Parsley, Chives or
Mint

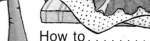

How to. . . . .

1. Put cabbage leaves, a few at a
time, into boiling water and cook
until just limp (they mustn't be
soggy). Lay on to
kitchen paper.

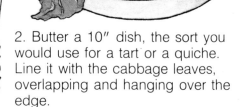

2. Butter a 10″ dish, the sort you
would use for a tart or a quiche.
Line it with the cabbage leaves,
overlapping and hanging over the
edge.

3. Put your 4 cups of vegetables in
a bowl. Then in another bowl,
beat eggs, add grated cheese, milk,
herbs and salt and pepper.
Pour over vegetables and mix.

20

4. Then pour everything into cabbage-lined dish and carefully fold over cabbage leaves so that the vegetables are completely enclosed — you may need an extra

couple of leaves on top.
Now bake at 375°F/180°C, Gas 5 for about 45 minutes.

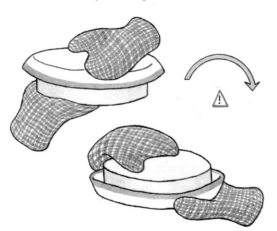

5. Get someone to help you turn it out on to a serving dish.

Delicious hot or cold.

Sort-of Shepherds' Pie

You will need........

4 tablespoons Rice
1 large Onion, chopped
1 tablespoon Oil
1 lb (448 g) Minced Beef
1 lb (448 g) Tomatoes
1 oz (28 g) Butter
1 oz (28 g) Flour
½ pint (300 ml) Milk
5 oz (140 g) grated Cheese
1 teaspoon Salt
½ teaspoon Pepper

How to........

1. Cook the onion in the oil over a low heat until it is soft (use a very large pan). Add the minced beef, cook until it is brownish looking.

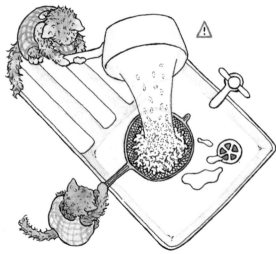

2. Chop the tomatoes and add those with the salt, pepper. Leave to simmer gently on a low heat for about 30 minutes.

3. In a large pan of boiling water, cook the rice until just tender and then drain.

22

4. In the saucepan that you cook the rice in, melt the butter, add the flour and mix well over a low heat.

5. Add the milk and keep stirring until the sauce is thick and smooth. Add 4 oz (102 g) grated cheese and stir until melted (add a dash of salt and pepper).

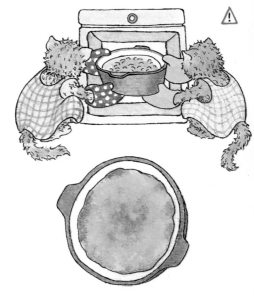

6. Spread half the meat mixture into an oven-proof dish, then spread the rice over this, then the rest of the meat, then pour the cheese sauce over the top and sprinkle 1 oz grated cheese on top of that.

7. Bake at 350°F/180°C, Gas 4 for 40 minutes until light brown and bubbling.

Fish Fish

You will need........

1 cup any Cooked Fish (flaked, no skin or bones)
1 cup mashed Potato
1 grated Carrot
1 Egg
Salt
Pepper
1 teaspoon of your favourite Herb

How to........

1. Mix till well blended.

2. Then make into fish shapes.

 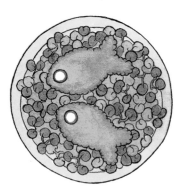

3. Melt together in a pan
1 dessertspoon oil and
1 dessertspoon butter.
Cook fish on both sides until lightly browned.

4. Serve on sea of chopped watercress. Make an 'eye' for the fish with a nut or piece of vegetable. Serves 2 – 4 (depending on the size of the fish).

Kedgeree

You will need........

12 oz (336 g) Cooked Fish (cod or kippers are nice)
8 oz (226 g) Rice
2 tablespoons Cream
2 oz (56 g) Butter
1 dessertspoon finely chopped Spring Onion
1 dessertspoon chopped Parsley or Chives
4 hard-boiled Eggs
Salt
Pepper

How to........

1. Make sure there are no skin or bones in the fish.

2. Cook the rice in plenty of boiling water until just tender.

3. Shell and chop eggs.
4. Melt butter, add onion and stir for 2 minutes.
Add drained rice with fish, salt and pepper and stir around.

5. Add the eggs, cream and herbs and keep stirring until everything is heated through.

Tuna Salad

You will need. . . . .

1 tin Tuna
3 or 4 Spring Onions, chopped
1 hard-boiled Egg, chopped
2 sticks Celery, chopped
2 heaped tablespoons Mayonnaise
1 red, dessert Apple, sliced

How to. . . . .

1. Drain tuna, put in large bowl and break up with a fork.
Add all other ingredients, mayonnaise last and mix gently.

2. Serve on lettuce or watercress (or fill a hamburger bun).

Sandwich Pie

You will need. . . . .

½ pint (300 ml) Milk
½ teaspoon Salt
¼ teaspoon Pepper
½ teaspoon Mustard Powder
6 slices Bread, buttered on both sides
3 slices Cheese, the same size as the bread
3 Eggs
(3 heaped teaspoons Chutney — if you like)

How to. . . . .

1. Place 3 slices of the buttered bread on a baking dish just large enough to hold them.
Place cheese on top of each slice. Spread each one with chutney. Then cover with the other slice of bread as if you were making a sandwich.

2. In a bowl, beat 3 eggs, milk, salt, pepper and mustard with a fork and then pour over the bread.

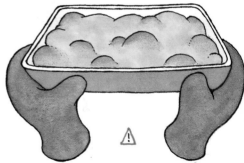

3. Bake at 300°F/160°C/Gas 2 for 30 minutes. Turn up heat to 325°F/170°C/Gas 3 for 15 minutes. Keep looking because it should be slightly brown and puffy.

Forget about it for about one hour.

Super Salad

You will need........

2 grated Carrots
2 sliced Tomatoes
3 sticks Celery (chopped or cut into strips)
1 Lettuce, (torn into pieces)
1 bunch of Watercress
6 Spring Onions
Handful Sultanas
4 oz (112 g) Raw Beetroot (grated)
4 oz (112 g) White Cabbage (sliced very thinly)

(The best salads are made with as many different vegetables as you can use — don't be afraid to experiment and add things like nuts and fruit — in fact, do your own thing.)

Here is one idea to start you off.

How to........

1. Wash and prepare everything. Put everything into a bowl except the beetroot.

2. Add your salad dressing. Then stir in the beetroot just before serving.

28

Simple Salad Dressing

You will need........

3 tablespoons Oil
1 tablespoon Vinegar
1 dessertspoon Honey
½ Lemon, squeezed
1 pinch Salt, to taste
1 pinch Pepper, to taste

How to........

Put in a jug, mix with a fork and add a heaped teaspoon of your favourite herb.

(Use orange juice instead of lemon, or add some plain yoghurt to make a creamy dressing.)

29

Cheese and Herb Show-off Souffle

You will need........

2 tablespoons Butter or Margarine
3 level tablespoons Flour
1 pint (600 ml) Milk
4 Egg Yolks
5 Egg Whites
4 oz (112 g) grated Cheese
(Cheddar or Cheshire)
½ teaspoon Salt
¼ teaspoon Pepper
1 teaspoon Worcestershire Sauce
1 dessertspoon chopped Parsley or
Chives (if using dried herbs, 1
teaspoonful)

Grease an oven-proof dish with straight sides.

How to........

1. Melt butter in a pan.
Stir in flour and blend well.
Take off heat, add milk gradually.
Put back on heat and keep stirring until mixture becomes like thick cream.

2. Take off the heat, stir in cheese, salt, pepper, Worcestershire sauce and herbs.

3. In a small bowl, beat egg yolks and then stir into mixture a little at a time.

4. In another bowl beat egg whites until stiff then gently fold these into the cheese mixture.

5. Pour into souffle dish.
Cook for about 30 minutes at 350°F/180°C, Gas 4 until lightly browned and well risen.
Serve immediately because souffles don't like to be kept waiting.

Unusual Burgers

You will need . . . .

4 oz (112 g) Red or Yellow Lentils
2 sticks Celery, chopped finely
1 large Carrot, grated
2 oz (56 g) White Cabbage, grated
or chopped
4 oz (112 g) Breadcrumbs
1 teaspoon Salt
½ teaspoon Pepper
2 Eggs

How to . . . .

1. Soak lentils in cold water
overnight (or for a few hours).
Rinse, then cook in boiling water
until just soft. Drain any remaining
water well.

2. Mix with everything, adding the
two beaten eggs last.
Make into hamburger shapes.

3. Heat a tablespoonful of oil in
frying pan and when hot, fry
burgers for a few minutes on each
side.

31

Beef Roll

You will need........

1½ lb (672 g) Minced Beef
2 Eggs
2 oz (56 g) Breadcrumbs
⅛ pint (75 ml) Tomato Sauce
2 tablespoons chopped Red,
Green or Yellow Pepper
2 tablespoons grated Carrot
2 oz (56 g) chopped Onion
½ teaspoon Salt
½ teaspoon Pepper
1 dessertspoon of your favourite
Herb
1 dessertspoon Worcestershire
Sauce

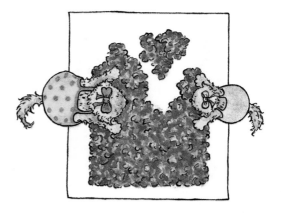

How to........

1. Mix everything except the beef in
a large bowl.
Then add beef and mix well.

2. Lay out a piece of waxed paper.
Turn beef mixture on to it and press
into an oblong shape measuring
about 10" × 8".

32

Now for the filling.
You will need........

About 8 oz (226 g) left-over
mashed Potato or 8 oz (226 g)
Cottage Cheese or 8 oz (226 g)
cooked Spinach or 8 oz (226 g)
mashed, cooked Carrot

1. Spread one of these fillings across the beef mixture

and then carefully lift the paper away from you, so that the meat flips over and rolls up.

2. When it looks like a Swiss roll, gently edge it on to a greased baking tin (seam side down if you can manage it. If not, pinch seam together with your fingers).
Bake at 350°F/180°C, Gas 4 for 40 to 45 minutes.

(This is delicious both hot and cold.)

Best Burgers

You will need........

½ lb (226 g) Minced Beef
2 tablespoons chopped Onion
2 tablespoons Tomato Ketchup
1 Carrot (grated)
4 oz (112 g) Breadcrumbs
½ teaspoon Salt
¼ teaspoon Pepper
1 teaspoon Worcestershire Sauce
2 tablespoons Salted Peanuts
(crushed a bit)
1 Egg

How to........

1. Mix everything together.

2. Take about 2 heaped tablespoons of the mixture (more or less won't matter) and pat into hamburger shape.

3. Heat 1 tablespoon oil in a frying pan.
When oil is hot put in 2 hamburgers. Brown gently on one side, then turn over and brown the other.
About 4 minutes each side should be right but it depends on the size of the hamburger and, of course, how you like them to be cooked.

4. Keep warm while you cook two more.

Serve in a bun or on lettuce with a salad or with a jacket potato.

Home-made Tomato Sauce

(Delicious on pasta or with beef roll or lots of other things)

You will need . . . .

1 medium Onion
5 large Tomatoes
½ teaspoon Salt
¼ teaspoon Pepper
1 stick of Celery
1 teaspoon Herbs (Basil, if you have some)

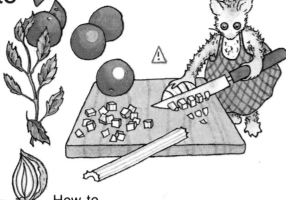

1 dessertspoon Brown Sugar
1 dessertspoon Butter
½ dessertspoon Oil

How to . . . .

1. Chop onion and celery very finely.

2. Melt butter and oil in pan. Add onion and celery and cook gently, stirring from time to time until the onion is soft. Add chopped tomatoes, salt, pepper, brown sugar and herbs.

3. Mix together and leave to simmer over very low heat for about ½ hour. Add a little water to thin, if necessary. Give it a stir now and again. Leave to get cool. You can use it as it is or put it in a blender to puree.

Quick Supper

You will need . . . .

4 oz (112 g) grated Carrot
2 oz (56 g) finely chopped Onion
4 oz (112 g) finely chopped Leeks
4 oz (112 g) Spinach (torn into small pieces)
2 sliced Tomatoes
½ teaspoon Salt
¼ teaspoon Pepper
4 oz (112 g) grated Cheese
2 Eggs
½ pint (300 ml) Milk

How to . . . .

1. Prepare all the vegetables, put in a bowl, stir in salt, pepper and grated cheese.

2. In another bowl, beat the eggs, add milk and pour over the vegetable mixture.

3. Lightly grease a baking dish and pour the mixture into it.
Bake at 350°F/180°C, Gas 4 for 40 minutes.

(Experiment with different combinations of vegetables.)

Fruit Crumble

You will need........

2 lb (896 g) Cooking Apples
(peeled and sliced)
1 Banana (sliced)
Small handful Sultanas
6 tablespoons Orange or Apple
Juice — put in a jug with 1
teaspoon Powdered Cinnamon,
1 heaped tablespoon Brown
Sugar (mix)

1. Put fruit and sultanas in a pie dish
and pour fruit juice mixture over them.

Crumble

You will need........

6 oz (168 g) Flour
3 oz (84 g) Butter
3 oz (84 g) Brown Sugar

How to........

1. Put in a bowl and mix with your
fingers (lightly) until it looks like
breadcrumbs. Sprinkle over fruit.
Bake for 20 minutes at 375°F/
180°C/ Gas 5.

2. Then have a look — the crumble
should look light brown and crunchy.
If you think it needs a little longer,
put it back in the oven for another 5
to 10 minutes and look again.

Carrot Pudding or Cake

You will need........

12 oz (336 g) Carrots
3 Egg Yolks
3 Egg Whites
8 oz (226 g) soft, dark Brown Sugar
6 oz (168 g) Ground Almonds
1 dessertspoon Orange Juice
1 tablespoon grated Orange Rind

Grease an 8″ dish (if you are making a pudding) or tin (if it is going to be a cake).

How to........

1. Cook peeled, sliced carrots in boiling water until very soft. Then puree in blender. When cold, measure out 6 oz of the puree.

2. Beat egg yolks until they are very pale. Add sugar and beat again. Add carrot puree, orange rind and orange juice and mix very well. Add ground almonds and mix again.

3. In another bowl, beat the egg whites until they are stiff, then fold them into the carrot mixture gently.

4. Bake at 325°F/170°C, Gas 3 for about 50 minutes.

To test if it is done, poke a skewer into the centre and if it comes out clean, it means it is ready. Serve warm for pudding or leave to get cold if serving as a cake.

Large Fruit Cake

You will need........
6 oz (168 g) Butter
6 oz (168 g) Sugar
3 Eggs
½ teaspoon each of ground Cinnamon, Ground Cloves and Nutmeg
12 oz (336 g) Self Raising Flour
12 oz (336 g) grated Carrot
8 oz (226 g) chopped Nuts
6 oz (168 g) Sultanas

How to........

1. In one bowl sift the flour with the cinnamon, cloves and nutmeg.

2. In another bowl, beat the sugar and butter together until pale and creamy.

3. Add the three eggs and beat those in.

4. Fold in the flour and add the carrot, chopped nuts and sultanas and mix all together.

5. Put into an 8″ well greased tin and bake at 325°F/170°C, Gas 3 for 1½ hours.

Honey Cake

You will need........

4 oz (113 g) Butter
2 oz (56 g) Sugar
3 tablespoons Honey (runny)
2 tablespoons Plain Yoghurt
2 beaten Eggs
8 oz (226 g) Flour, sifted with
3 teaspoons Baking Powder

How to........

1: Cream butter and sugar together *thoroughly.*

2. Then mix in honey, beating well.
Add 2 beaten eggs, beat again.
Add 2 tablespoons yoghurt,
beat again.

3. Add sifted flour and baking powder. Mix.

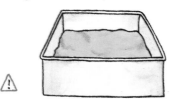

4. Spoon into greased 7″ (17.5cm) cake tin.
5. Bake at 350°F/180°C, Gas 4 for about 45 minutes.

(Serve spread with butter.)

40

Bears' Biscuits

You will need........

4 oz (112 g) Butter
4 oz (112 g) Grated Coconut
4 oz (112 g) Sugar
4 oz (112 g) Ground Rice
2 oz (56 g) Cornflour

How to........

1. Mix everything together, until it drops off the spoon.

2. If it doesn't, add a little milk, but not too much. Drop from a teaspoon into mounds on a greased baking sheet, well spaced out.

3. Bake at 350°F/180°C, Gas 4 until light brown.

4. Remove from tray when still warm, but set firm.

Makes about 18.

Chocolate Cake for a Special Occasion

You will need........

6 oz (168 g) Plain Chocolate
4 oz (112 g) Butter
4 oz (112 g) Sugar
1½ oz (42 g) Cornflour
4 Eggs (separated)
2 oz (56 g) Ground Almonds

How to........

1. Break up the chocolate and put it in a small saucepan and stand it in a larger saucepan containing very hot water. Put on a low heat and watch it melt, stirring.

2. Put butter in a large bowl and beat until smooth. Add sugar and beat again.

3. Add cornflour and add egg yolks, one at a time. Keep beating until everything is well mixed. Add ground almonds and beat again. Add the melted chocolate and mix until everything is well blended.

4. In another bowl, beat the egg whites until they are stiff and then fold them into the chocolate mixture.

5. Do this gently with a metal spoon, folding everything together until no white shows.

6. Put into a greased cake tin, about 8″, and bake for 45 minutes at 350°F/180°C/Gas 4, (test with a skewer to see if it is done).

Special Home-made Ice-cream

You will need........

½ pint (300 ml) Double Cream
4 oz (112 ml) Brown Breadcrumbs
8 oz (226 g) Brown Sugar
1 tablespoon Honey
Grated rind of 1 large Orange

How to........

1. Beat cream until thick, adding honey as you do it. Stir in the orange rind. Put into a container. Cover and then put into the freezer compartment of the fridge.

2. Mix breadcrumbs with sugar and sprinkle on to a very lightly oiled baking tin. Bake at 375°F/180°C, Gas 5, until brown and crunchy.

3. Take them out every few minutes and stir so that all the crumbs get brown. (These burn very easily so don't leave the oven).

4. When the crumbs are cold, remove the cream mixture from the freezer, stir in breadcrumbs, cover and return to freezer until frozen.

Chocolate Chip Cheesecake

You will need........

Crust
4 oz (112 g) Digestive Biscuits (crushed)
2 oz (56 g) Butter
1 dessertspoon Sugar

Filling
1 lb (448 g) Philadelphia Cream Cheese
3 oz (84 g) Sugar
2 Eggs
3 – 4 oz (100g) Chocolate Chips
Small carton Double or Whipping Cream

How to........

Crust

1. Melt butter gently over a low heat.

2. Add crushed biscuits and sugar.

3. Stir and then press into the bottom of a tin (a spring-based tin is best, about 8″ across but don't worry if it's not quite the right size).

Filling

1. In large bowl with electric mixer, if possible, beat cream cheese and cream until smooth.

2. Beat in eggs and sugar really well.

3. Then stir in chocolate chips, pour into tin. Bake in the oven for 45 minutes at 375°F/180°C, Gas 5. Leave to get cold (You can sprinkle with chocolate flakes if you wish.)

This is a very large, delicious cheesecake to make for a special occasion and it serves up to 8 – 10 people.

(You can halve this recipe if you want to.)

45

Apple Banana Bread

You will need........

8 oz (226 g) Wholewheat Flour
2 Ripe Bananas
1 small Eating Apple (peeled and chopped)
½ teaspoon Salt
1½ teaspoons Baking Powder
4 tablespoons Plain Yoghurt
1 Egg
8 oz (226 g) Brown Sugar
4 oz (112 g) Butter

How to........

1. Beat the butter and sugar together until really well mixed. Beat in the egg. Then mash the bananas and mix them in.

2. Mix the flour, baking powder and salt. Mix half the yoghurt into the banana mixture. Then add half the flour, then the rest of the yoghurt, then the rest of the flour and fold well together.

3. Add the apple and fold that in.

4. Grease a loaf tin, put in mixture. Bake at 350°F/180°C, Gas 4 for 1 hour.

Weights and Measures Dept.

1oz Butter, Margarine or Fat	= **28 grams**	= 2 level tablespoons
1oz Brown Sugar	= **28 grams**	= 2 level tablespoons
1oz Wholewheat Flour	= **28 grams**	= 3 level tablespoons
1oz Grated Cheese	= **28 grams**	= 4 level tablespoons
1oz Rice	= **28 grams**	= 1½ level tablespoons
1oz Currants, Raisins	= **28 grams**	= 2 level tablespoons
1 pint (20 fl. ozs.) Liquid	= **600 ml**	
2 teaspoons	= **1 dessertspoon**	
2 dessertspoons	= **1 tablespoon**	

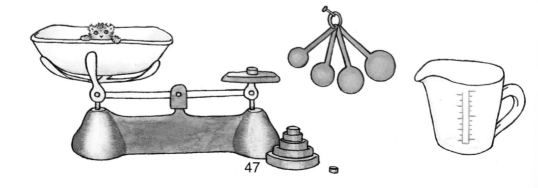

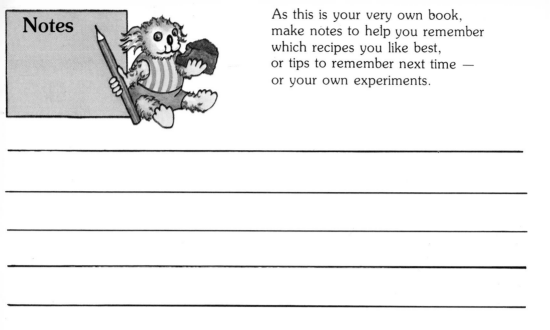

Notes

As this is your very own book, make notes to help you remember which recipes you like best, or tips to remember next time — or your own experiments.

Acknowledgement
Rear cover photograph by kind permission of Terry O'Neill.